Saved,
Now What?

A Guide for the New Believer

Jahred & Rukiya Rice

For information regarding special discounts for bulk purchases contact the Publisher:

LaBoo Publishing Enterprise, LLC
staff@laboopublishing.com
www.laboopublishing.com

All information is solely considered as the point of view of the authors.

Table of Contents

Introduction

Saved From What?

What does it mean to be saved? What does it mean to confess Jesus as Lord and Savior? If someone genuinely asked you what you believe, why do you believe it, and how does that impact your life, could you confidently answer that question? Tough questions, right? Many believers and Christians around the world also have trouble answering these questions. In most cases, it is by no means their own fault. Unfortunately, these hallmark questions, these foundations of the Christian faith and experience are largely unanswered by the existing body of Christ. It is safe to say millions of people every year convert to Christianity. Millions of people every year make a courageous walk down to the altar or stage at a church and repeat a prayer of salvation or what some call the "sinner's prayer". However, while the Spirit of God led them to do so, their minds have yet to fully understand what exactly they've just done. Furthermore, through our experience, we have also seen another dire question that most new converts or new believers, and even some lifelong believers who are rededicating themselves back to God, need an answer to. That question is, "Now that I am saved, now what?"

We have encountered and met many new believers who have given their lives to Christ and the main questions they ask us falls along the lines of, "Where do I start? What do I need to do now that I'm saved? What books of the Bible should I read? Should I join a church? What church should I join? Does this mean I have to become a preacher now? Do I have to work at church? Do I have to stop listening to music? How do I know I'm praying correctly?" We've heard them all.

We hope this book will help answer many questions that new and seasoned believers have never gotten answers to, along with the wisdom of the Holy Spirit, and the insight and knowledge found and revealed from the scriptures of the Holy Bible. In some cases, our hope in God is that where understanding may be incomplete that we may step into the "whole counsel of God" according to Acts 20:27 (NKJV) concerning matters of salvation and what to do after we have made that monumental decision to follow Jesus Christ. As you read this book, we encourage you to take notes, highlight, underline, and do whatever else helps you thoroughly comprehend the contents of this book. We pray that by the end of this book, you will gain assurance in your salvation and confidence to take the steps to begin your walk with Christ that leads to maturity in Christ and a life of excellence.

Chapter 1

What Do We Believe?
The Principles of Faith

What do we believe as Christians?

Christianity is grounded in the life, death, and resurrection of Jesus Christ. We believe that we have all been born into and shaped in sin and because of this sin, we have been separated from God not only on earth but eternally. Sin entered into the life of man when Adam and Eve disobeyed God through eating from a tree that was forbidden for them to eat from. Eve was enticed and convinced by the serpent that this tree could surely be eaten without the consequence of death and, in turn, she encouraged her husband Adam to partake in the eating of the fruit from that tree. This tree that they ate from was located in the Garden of Eden. Eden was known as the presence of God, which is where God placed Adam and Eve to fellowship with Him always. Due to the disobedience of one man, the nature of sin was birthed to all men, including you and me.

What is Sin?

Sin simply means to miss the mark. Now, if we look at the mark or standard that we have missed, it's the righteousness of God. Righteousness means to be in right standing with God. Before the life, death and resurrection of Jesus, attempts to reclaim righteousness were done through the sacrifice of animals before God through a qualified priest. Men and women did not have the luxury of going before God boldly and laying requests before Him. Imagine always needing a middleman to ensure your forgiveness and your needs are met. This is what sin did to us in proximity to God. We could no longer approach Him, and there was a continuous divide. Sin continued to take root in the hearts of man, pulling us further away from God. In the stories of old, God exercised His wrath to men, cities, and generational lines because of sin. Priests were killed in the presence of God if they were not found to be holy and blameless. Sin caused God's mercies to be displayed as He pleased. Do you get the picture? This thing called sin has caused mankind to be separated from God's goodness and mercy.

Why do we need to be saved?

It was the plan of the serpent to separate Adam and Eve from the presence of God, to separate them from constant communion with their father. Satan's plan has not changed much at all. His aim is to continue to keep us from God. As an ex-angel, he understands the great reward and benefits from being with God forever and being unable to return to his place in God's presence; he wants our destiny to look like his with eternal damnation and eternal suffering.

God's love plan for us

While sin came through one man (Adam), God in his sovereignty and His great love for us, allowed salvation and reconnection back to Him come through one man— Jesus Christ. God so loved the world that He sent His only begotten son to us, that whoever would believe in him, shouldn't perish in this life but would be granted life more abundantly here and eternally. John 3:16, which I just quoted, depicts two very important things in the Christian faith. The first thing explains why we need saving. John 3:16 tells us that because of our belief in the one God has sent, we do not perish. This means life apart from Jesus is a life that is wasting away both now and forever. The second thing John 3:16 tells us is that it is because God loved us that He sent a piece of himself (His son) to dwell amongst us and die for us. This love for us came with a price, and that price was that His son would become the ultimate sacrificial lamb. Thanks to this, we would no longer need middlemen or priests to sacrifice animals for us in order to be forgiven and commune with Him. Christians believe and know that because of this sacrifice we have been given salvation and are now exempt from God's righteous judgment. Salvation takes us out of the darkness and chains of sin and back into the place of Eden with God, both now and forever.

The simplest way to explain this and the essence of salvation would be to give you an analogy. Imagine you have an incredibly wealthy friend and this friend owns a really fancy restaurant. You tell him one day you want to go and eat at this restaurant and he agrees and tells you to meet him there. The time comes and you go to the restaurant and you end up arriving before he does and are seated alone. Now some time has passed, and he still hasn't shown up, so you decide to just order your food. You order the most expensive things on the menu, creating an enormous bill. Now when you finish your meal, your friend still hasn't shown up, and the waiter comes and requests you pay your bill. You didn't bring any money to cover the bill because your friend invited you, so you expected it to be covered. So now you are left in a tight spot; you haven't seen or heard from your friend and you have no money and cannot leave unless the bill is paid. Just when you are getting extremely worried, and the restaurant staff begin to grow impatient, in walks your friend. He approaches the table and tells the waiter not to worry about the bill, as it is all on him. He then takes you by the hand and leads you out of the restaurant with no issue.

In this story, the restaurant is the world and hell. The waiter is death. The food you had is sin. As for your friend? Your friend is Jesus. When you were in the world, destined for hell because of the debt you inherited through sin, death came to collect that debt. Fortunately, Jesus came and paid the bill for you just in time. He took on all your debts and walked you out of hell into safety. This is salvation. This is the love God showed us through the substitutionary sacrifice of Jesus. This is what we believe.

Chapter 2

Your Personal Walk
With God

As a believer, it is important to understand that salvation and receiving Jesus as your personal Lord and Savior is step one. Now that you have given your life to Christ, it's important to know that it is a lifelong journey. This is a journey of progression to fully get to a place where, not only is your eternal positioning (your place in heaven) secured, but one that now molds you to becoming all that God created you to be. Being all that God created you to be is about our purpose, calling, contribution to the body of Christ and the world, and effectiveness in representing Kingdom principles and helping a dying world understand Jesus' sacrifice for humanity. In order to achieve these things, it will take a strategic and methodical approach to how you now do this thing called life.

Many believers come to the saving knowledge of Christ but have no one to show them the next steps or disciple them into maturity in Christ. Many revert to the things we heard about before, such as going to church every Sunday or consistently attending church events; trying to piece together what we saw from various sources. But God is not a God of guess work. When you look through scripture, especially in the books of Genesis and even Exodus, you will see the characteristic of just how meticulous and calculated God is. Let's take a deeper look. In Genesis chapter one, we have the Creation story that so elegantly gives us a peek into the mind of God. Starting from verse three all the way to verse 31, we see God's careful method of creating, analyzing, critiquing, and then confirming. This was a process that He would continue throughout the next few chapters of Genesis. If we are made in His image, we must also be calculated about how we grow spiritually, how we grow our relationship with Jesus, and how we grow holistically within our everyday lives.

I want to give a few keys that I have found to be extremely helpful as a new believer and even some more seasoned believers who maybe haven't had the opportunity to hear them. They will help in cultivating a healthy and prosperous walk with Christ, and serve as a great jumping off point for us as we begin this new and exciting journey with Christ.

1. Prayer

Prayer is the absolute lifeline of any and every believer. There is no way around prayer if you want to live an excelling life with God. Prayer is not something that can be substituted or neglected; it is one of the things that every believer MUST do and do well. Luke 18:1 (KJV) says, "And he spake a parable unto them to this end, that men ought always to pray, and not to faint." Matthew 6:6 (NIV) says, "But when you pray, go into your room, close the door and pray to your Father, who is unseen. Then your Father, who sees what is done in secret, will reward you."

In these texts, Jesus is speaking to the disciples (His followers) and teaching them about prayer. A very important component of what Jesus was saying is that prayer is mandatory. The text in Matthew says, "when you pray," which means it is not a matter of if you pray, but the amount of time you do. In Luke 18:1, Jesus answers the question of when, saying, "men ought always to pray." So, these two scriptures now begin to highlight to us just how monumental prayer is for the believer. Prayer is not just a means to gain things from God or to change circumstances; even though prayer can result in those things, it shouldn't be our main motivation in prayer. The number one goal of prayer is TRANSFORMATION; changing and aligning ourselves daily to look more like Christ and His kingdom programming.

What is prayer? Prayer is our communication with God. Prayer serves many different purposes, which we will get into a little later on, but at its core, it is how we connect to God. It is our telephone to God. In the Garden of Eden with Adam and Eve, there was no prayer. Why? Because they were already in the presence of God and there was nothing separating them from God. Prayer was introduced after the fall of man because the nature of sin disconnected us from God, so there now had to be some sort of vehicle or mode in which we could communicate with God. That vehicle is prayer. When we speak about prayer, we must understand the way it works and why it is so important, and to do that, we must understand the dominion mandate. The dominion mandate is what God gave man when He created him in the Garden of Eden. This is outlined in Genesis 2:5, 2:15, and 2:19.

Through his craftiness, Satan tricked Adam and Eve into turning over that dominion to him through the fall of man (Genesis 3). This is important to know because one of the purposes of prayer is to get God to legally operate and intervene in the affairs of man and earth. This is because legally God gave up that dominion, and God isn't one to go back on His word. He's also a God of principle. With that being said, we must now jump ahead yet again to Jesus coming and dying for us so that our sins be forgiven and so we can be restored back to the Father. When Jesus died, He went to hell and defeated all the powers of Satan and took back the keys of authority and dominion over the heavens and the earth. Matthew 28:18 (NKJV) says, "And Jesus came and spoke to them, saying, 'All authority has been given to Me in heaven and on earth.'"

So we now understand that through Jesus' sacrifice and resurrection, He has all power and authority, but then we see something very interesting happen and be beneficial for us. Luke 10:18-20 (NKJV) says, And He said to them, "I saw Satan fall like lightning from heaven. Behold, I give you the authority to trample on serpents and scorpions, and over all the power of the enemy, and nothing shall by any means hurt you. Nevertheless, do not rejoice in this, that the spirits are subject to you, but rather rejoice because your names are written in heaven." This is a good place to gently sit this book down and run around wherever you are! Jesus says He saw Satan fall, then He gave us authority over ALL the power of the enemy! That means that the dominion and the authority that were once stolen from us have now been restored back to us.

So, with this in mind, I want to tell you that prayer is you now exercising your legal right, dominion, and authority to call upon the God of heaven to make any and everything that doesn't align or look like the will of God for your life to be corrected through prayer. We position ourselves to the heart of God and begin to re-write every evil thing that has taken place in our lives and legislate the correct things, which is the will of God for us. As a believer, prayer is your superpower, so never neglect it.

How to pray?

I want to give a simple yet highly effective way to pray, and this is not my own theology, but it is the way Jesus teaches us to pray. This approach to prayer can be found in Matthew 6:9-13 (NKJV):

> After this manner therefore pray ye:
>
> Our Father which art in heaven, Hallowed be thy name.
>
> Thy kingdom come, Thy will be done in earth, as it is in heaven.
>
> Give us this day our daily bread.
>
> And forgive us our debts, as we forgive our debtors.
>
> And lead us not into temptation, but deliver us from evil: For thine is the kingdom, and the power, and the glory, forever. Amen.

This is the model Jesus gave us and, at face value, it's easy to take this prayer and pray it quite literally. I was taught this prayer when I was growing up, but did not really understand what it meant. I knew it was the Lord's Prayer, so I should know it. It wasn't until recently that I gained an understanding of this specific prayer and why Jesus instructed us in this way. The first thing I would like to point out is verse nine, where He says to pray in this manner, not pray this word for word. That means that the prayer itself wasn't meant to be prayed verbatim, but used as a template. Let's break this down now and see if we can now understand how we should mold our prayers.

"Our Father which art in heaven:" This line tells us to whom we are praying, as well as His position and authority. By understanding this, we are acknowledging that God is above and outside of our circumstance and so He has the ability to answer and intervene as need be.

"Hallowed be thy name:" The definition of hallowed in this verse means "to be greatly revered and honored." By praying this, we have now come to a place of honor for God, but not only that when you honor His name, you are also honoring the power, authority, and dominion that His name carries. Think about any president of the United States you know, even when they are no longer in office. They are still honored, but why? Because the power they hold that demands honor was not in their first and last name, but in the name of the office they occupied. That honor you give to God, whose name is above every other name, now authorizes Him to begin to move in the dimension of power that is attached to his position.

"Thy kingdom come, thy will be done, on earth, as it is in heaven:" In any kingdom there is a king and that king establishes rules, principles, and the overall standard by which life is to be lived within that territory. As a believer, we must understand that we are citizens of God's kingdom first before we are a citizen of any nation or country here on earth. With that being said, to pray that God's kingdom comes and His will be done here on earth as it is in heaven is saying that our desires are that whatever He has for us in this life are in accordance with His will and principles.

"Give us this day our daily bread:" Now that you have acknowledged the Father and His position, authority, will, and principles to be established in your life, we now ask and receive daily provision for the day. There is a name synonymous with God that you may have heard: "Abba". The word Abba stands for Father and is also defined as "the source" and "sustainer". When we pray for daily bread, we are pulling on the Father, the source, the sustainer dimension of God that He may now look into our days and supply all of our needs. This includes anything from peace to joy, food, money, resources, and more.

"Forgive us our debts, as we forgive our debtors:" We pray that the Lord would forgive us because, as we have learned, we were born in sin and we still live within a fleshly body and we forever need the Lord to show us mercy. But it is important to know that we cannot obtain that forgiveness from God and yet still hold any unforgiveness towards anyone else. One negates the other, so when we pray we are not only obtaining forgiveness, but we are also releasing the unforgiveness we have towards anyone else.

"And lead us not into temptation, but deliver us from evil:" We understand that there will be many temptations that try to pull us away from God, His will, and His presence so we ask the Lord to give us the grace to overcome those temptations and live solely for God and not be partakers in evil.

"For thine is the kingdom, and the power, and the glory, forever. Amen:" We end our prayers once again, acknowledging God and showing reverence and thankfulness to the fact that He is above all and He will be the King of Kings and Lord of Lords forever.

When we approach prayer knowing its importance, and go into it with the model laid out to us by Jesus, we now have the key to transform our entire life to make it look like Christ. That is the overall goal of prayer. Prayer is not something you do every once in a while, but as you start, even in small increments, over time your capacity increases and you will see the incredible effect prayer has in the life of the believer. When you read Acts 4:6, you will find that it takes continuity and consistency in the place of prayer that brings maturity and growth for believers. The scripture reads, "But we will give ourselves continually to prayer, and to the ministry of the word." Now that we understand the importance of prayer, we must also know that prayer alone will leave us grossly imbalanced, and so, according to this scripture, there is yet another component that is absolutely necessary for every believer. That is the Word of God.

2. The Word of God (Holy Bible)

John 1:1 (NKJV) says, "In the beginning was the Word, and the Word was with God, and the Word was God." Before we even begin to talk about the importance of the Word, the most important thing that we absolutely must know is that the Word of God IS GOD. When you understand that, then you automatically have a better understanding and appreciation of the Word. The Word of God serves many purposes that all ultimately lead to us excelling in life. The Word of God is the backbone for every believer. The Word of God thoroughly outlines the extent of God's commitment to the believer in any and every aspect of life, both physically and spiritually. Psalm 138:2 says, "For thou hast magnified thy word above all thy name." God's word is the only thing above God. The Word of God is the most powerful thing in all of existence. Our world, our humanity, and all we know, both the seen and unseen, were formed by God's Word. His word is the only thing that will be left standing that you rest assured in and have full confidence in when all else fails in life. So what are some of the different purposes of the word?

- The Word of God shows us who God is. It is impossible to truly develop a love relationship with someone you do not know. The word of God allows us to see God's character, His intentions, His purposes, the things He loves, things He hates, and also the extent of His love for us. The word of God shows us also the various names and functions God goes by. All this information allows us to establish and deepen our love relationship with God.

- The Word of God shows us who WE are. Within the Bible, you can find God's design, His intent, and His hope for humanity. As you continue to dive deep into the Old Testament and New Testament, you'll find just who God has designed you to be. You begin to realize that your identity was to be and is to be defined by the one who created you and not by the world you live in. An example of finding this identity can be seen in the book of Jeremiah chapter one, verse five, "Before I formed you in the womb I knew you, before you were born I set you apart; I appointed you as a prophet to the nations." Here we see that even before our earthly conception, God already had an identity for us and a plan! When you begin to submit yourself to the word of God, you begin to allow God to reveal to you who you were always intended to be. When you dive even further, you begin to also realize that everything we are to be is found in Jesus Christ. In Hebrews chapter one, Jesus is described as the "express image of God, the brightness of His glory." Romans 8:29 says, "For whom he did foreknow, he also did predestinate to be conformed to the image of his Son, that he might be the firstborn among many brethren." These two verses show us that it is our purpose to become like Christ, that our identity rests upon our likeness to Christ, and if Christ is the brightness of the glory of God and the express image of God, then that should be our identity here on earth. Our identity should be so much in Christ that when people look at our life, character, and the content of our words/heart, they should see God.

- The Word of God contains the promises of God. These promises are the extent of God's commitment to act in the lives of believers. These promises are what allow us to walk in daily assurance and power. The knowledge of these promises is the basis of our hope in life. Research lets us know that there are over 7,000 written promises in the Bible, all of which we can stand on in our daily lives. A promise is defined as a declaration or assurance that one will do a particular thing or that a particular thing will happen. With this understanding, anywhere you see God speak in the Bible and declare a thing to a man or make an oath, covenant, or swear to do or not to do something qualifies as a promise. Through faith, we can utilize and stand on these promises.

There is so much more to speak about when considering the purpose of the Word of God, but these are just a few key points. I pray that these be a good starting point in your understanding of the importance of the Word of God and its necessity in our lives as believers. Other purposes of the Word of God that I will challenge you to find on your own are prophecy, instruction, kingdom principles, and revelation. All of these purposes are equally important and needed to acquire the full counsel of God for a fulfilling and excelling life in Christ. I encourage you to start small and then allow the Holy Spirit to drive you deeper as you grow in your walk. Begin by submitting to a bible plan, which you can find on apps like the Bible App, or I recommend starting with learning, studying, and knowing everything the Bible says about our Lord and Savior, Jesus Christ. You can find the epitome of His life and ministry in the gospels (the first four books of the New Testament). These books include Matthew, Mark, Luke, and John. This is a great place to start because Jesus is the start of our faith. After you study these, or in tandem with studying these, I would recommend reading the book of Psalms. This book was written by a man named David and will show you a vulnerability and intimacy with God that we all, as believers, should desire to have with our creator.

Cultivating your walk in Christ is a lifelong and ongoing process that you'll never fully complete, but it is absolutely mandatory. By devoting yourself in this way to your growth, you have positioned yourself in a way that allows for your consistent growth, both spiritually and in the natural. We must say that as you are growing in Christ, it is important to not set yourself back by going back and sinning. Keep yourself pure, away from temptations of all sorts, and constantly asking the Lord to show us mercy. If we can develop a lifestyle that is consistent in our devotion to the Word of God and prayer, the possibilities and the assurance of a wonderful, purposeful, and excelling life are endless. When we input these as the pillars of our Christian experience, God will undoubtedly look to use us in mighty ways as well as make our lives as signs and wonders to win even more people to the saving knowledge of Christ and the advancement of His Kingdom. Finally, when you cultivate your walk in this way, it does not negate the presence of struggle or problems, but it does ensure you are not going at it alone, but yet you have the backing, wisdom, and guidance of God. In any and every situation, you have an assurance that it will work for your good. The moment you cultivate your walk with God and dedicate yourself to this growth, God will make your life into something magnificent that you never could even imagine. Get ready! God is about to blow your mind!

Chapter 3

Discipleship

Within the span of his three-year ministry, Jesus was known for discipling 12 men, teaching them, training them, and equipping them to spread the gospel of Jesus and the Kingdom of Heaven. Through the scriptures we see Jesus traveling with the 12, teaching them through real-world examples and parables, and also empowering them to do the same miracles, signs, and wonders which He did. As we follow their stories, we see that they become the first apostles and were sent out after Jesus rose from the grave and ascended into heaven to go out into all the world and bring salvation to anyone who would believe. Having this understanding, we must now know that just as Jesus' disciples went through the process of discipleship with him, we must also go through that same process. Now, while Jesus is no longer physically here in a natural body, we still have the ability to be discipled by Him through the men and women whom He equips and anoints for the work. In every case, we choose to sit under and learn from a man of God or woman of God who will methodically nurture us in our growth to become mature believers and witnesses unto Christ.

What is discipleship?

Discipleship in one word means "following." To be a disciple is to be a follower. The question is what or who are you following. Let's take the first 12 disciples of Jesus as a case study. Matthew 4:18-20 and Mark 1:16-18 both describe how the first disciples came to be; Jesus called Simon (Peter) and Andrew to come and follow him. While this small piece of information may seem minute in importance, it actually carries key insight into what it means to be a disciple, and ultimately what discipleship is all about. Based on these two passages, the very first thing that makes you a disciple is not how you follow, but it is your being called. The first thing that happens is that Jesus called them. As a believer, there are two calls we should know about and focus on for the sake of this topic. Number one is the call you received from God that led to your salvation. This is undoubtedly the first and most important call of all, and likely the reason you are reading this book. The second call, which we want to focus on, is the who to follow or be discipled by.

In this land of discipleship, you must be called. After you have recognized and answered the call comes the following. The Bible lets us know that after Simon and Andrew were called, they immediately went and followed Jesus. There are a few dictionary definitions that I would like us to know that define the word "follow". The dictionary defines follow as "to act according to," "pay close attention to," "to practice," and "to conform to". All of these definitions are exactly what we need to know as it relates to following Christ and discipleship as a whole.

As a believer, our job, once we have been saved, is to pay close attention to the ways, principles, and teachings of Jesus so that we may now conform, practice, act, or live according to the godly standard that has been demonstrated in the life of Jesus and set before us to partake in. In this walk with Christ, as you follow Him, and conform to His will and His ways, you aren't losing yourself; in fact, you are losing all the old you and finally finding the true you. Think about it. You were made to be in perfect fellowship with God as His child, but you were born into a world that hates God and wants to strip you of your true identity. Now that you've finally made your way back home, it's time to take off the dirty clothes and put on your clean ones. This is the goal of discipleship. It is leading you back from the darkness into God's desired light for your life.

Now, while folks like Simon, Andrew, Matthew, and the rest of the 12 had the privilege of physically walking with Jesus, we must realize we don't have that luxury. But God, in His infinite wisdom, accounted for that and raised up men and women of God who we can trust to lead us, teach us, and guide us in the ways of Jesus. The Apostle Paul so beautifully stated to the church of Corinth, in 1 Corinthians 11:1 (KJV), "Follow me, as I follow Christ." This is the epitome of discipleship today. This reintroduces the concept of calling again. Not everyone is called to follow and not everyone has been called to disciple you, but do know there is someone for everyone. One reason many new believers fall away from the faith is because they have not found or held on to someone who can genuinely walk them through the process of starting this walk with Christ. Now, I am not one to talk negatively about God's people, but unfortunately, the body of Christ has fallen short in this area of disciplining new believers. In most cases, new believers get thrown into a church where they don't know anything or anybody, where no one is teaching them the ABCs of Christianity and the faith. Then, when they fall back into sin and their old ways, the church then turns their nose down at them and sometimes rejects them yet again, as if it was their fault they didn't pursue God or as if they were not serious. Actually, they heard the cry of the Holy Spirit, tried climbing out of the pit that is the world, and nobody grabbed their hand to help them out.

Chapter 3

This is the sad reality that must change if we are going to see an excelling and spotless bride on the day of the Lord's return. The way that we do this is what we've been talking about this entire chapter: discipleship.

As a new believer, you should desire discipleship and mentorship. You should pray that the Lord sends someone into your life that will diligently help train you up in the things of God. While you wait for that person, you still have the ability to be mentored from afar. As you go down this walk with Christ, you'll begin to realize that the Lord will allow you to come across certain men and women of God whose sound grace and ministry may touch your heart in a unique way. Now, this isn't talking about pastors or preachers who tickle your ear by saying all the things you love to hear, and make you comfortable, but instead make something inside of you leap through their teaching or declarations. This is similar to how John leaped in the womb of Elizabeth when Mary, pregnant with Jesus, came to visit. This is when something within you knows that this is a grace you need in your life. In some cases, the Lord may give you dreams or visions of men/women of God whom you may or may not have heard of before, draw you toward their ministry or teachings to impart a particular grace, or lead you to the specific type of training you need. As you begin to be mentored both personally and from afar, always remember that the best disciple is one who is always teachable

31

at every level and always takes the position of knowing that they know not as they ought to know, as stated in 1 Corinthians 8:2.

As you venture down the road of discipleship, always be sure that the ones you are following are always following Jesus. As mentioned in 1 Corinthians 11:1, "Follow me, as I follow Christ." The ultimate goal of discipleship and in the life of every believer is to know Jesus, to become like Him, and become His ambassador here on earth in every aspect of our lives so that His purposes are made manifest.

Chapter 4

The Church and Godly Community

One of the costliest things that happens when someone gives their life to Christ, is that they step into salvation but have no godly community to surround them and help them in this new life. In nature, for example, let's take the lion. When a lion gives birth to a brand-new cub, the cub will stay very close to their mother. This typically lasts for about six months. From then to about the age of three, in the case of male cubs, they stick with the lion pride until they have reached maturity and are able to go out and find their own pride and fend for themselves. I find this case study very interesting because it shows us quite a few lessons. The first being that anytime a person is newly introduced into the body of Christ, there must be a community that is built around them. Without such a community, that babe or brand-new cub is easy prey for any predator lurking around for an easy meal. When someone first gives their life to Christ, they are typically still walking around in a world surrounded by other people who have yet to receive salvation and this newness of life, which can make it very easy for them to fall back into the darkness from which they were just saved.

To add to that we must also be aware that a person receiving the salvation of Christ is the absolute last thing the devil wants, and so you must be vigilant and know that while they are still brand new he will try to sway them back into their old, dead life. The second lesson we can take from the lions is that in most cases it takes about six months to understand a new life and then three years to reach a level of maturity in which one can begin to fend for themselves and then go out and create a thriving life.

This pattern sounds very familiar to me, but does it sound familiar to you? If you begin to think about Jesus and the disciples, then you are right on target. Jesus began His ministry at the age of 30. Then He began to recruit His disciples and completed His ministry on earth by the age of 33. In those three years, we saw the strategic mentorship, training, and maturing of the disciples. They had formed a community of brotherhood built of faith and trust, not only on Jesus but also on one another. As they each grew in this community, they were sent out after three years to do the great work of their lives and fulfill their purpose. Through those lessons they learned from

Jesus and with each other, we see the formation of the first church in the book of Acts.

Having the right people around you is a fundamental law in life. There's a saying, "If you are in a room with nine foolish people, then unfortunately you may not have counted correctly, because there are 10 foolish people, you, being the tenth." This basically means that you are a direct product of those you are surrounded by. The same is true for us believers; as we have been translated into light, it is important that we surround ourselves with light, or else we may end up falling right back into darkness. With this understanding, we start to begin to realize the necessity for what we call the church.

What is church? The church can be defined simply as the body of Christ; anyone who has accepted Jesus as their Lord and personal savior has been engrafted into the body of Christ AKA the church. The church is not limited to a building, but is the very people, the community that believers have formed, who gather in the name of Jesus Christ. The church is also a training ground. The church is an educational institution designed to teach, grow, and equip the people of God to become passionate and effective witnesses of Jesus Christ. It is the system that God himself designed to teach us the principles and keys of the kingdom of God, and how to superimpose those realities here on earth. Matthew 18:20 (NKJV) says, "For where two or three are gathered together in My name, I am there in the midst of them." Anywhere two or more believers gather in any place, Jesus is there, and in that place is church. As a new believer, being a part of a biblically sound, bible believing, Holy Spirit filled church is paramount in your growth moving forward. In many cities in the United States of America, you will find many church buildings but very few genuine churches. The genuine indication of a true church is the outright acknowledgment that Jesus is Lord, sound biblical doctrine is being taught, and the tangible presence of the Holy Spirit is there.

The importance of a good church and godly community in the life of a new believer cannot be stressed enough. These two pillars in a believer's life not only help them to mature but also act as a safe haven and a protection. In the Bible, let's look at how vital the role of church and community is. In Acts 12, King Herod arrested the Apostle Peter. At this time, many believers of Jesus were being arrested, persecuted, and even killed for sharing the gospel. Peter was arrested and was waiting for the king to kill him. Acts 12:5 (NKJV) says, "Peter was therefore kept in prison, but constant prayer was offered to God for him by the church." The church, and their fellow brothers and sisters, began to pray and stand on behalf of the imprisoned Peter. Later, an angel of God came and, in a brazen prison escape, rescued Peter from prison and death. The value of being a part of a church and having a godly community can never be quantified.

The church is one of our lifelines as believers. If you are a believer in Jesus and not a part of an on-fire church and community, you are playing at a huge disadvantage and leaving yourself very vulnerable to attack from the enemy. If you've ever watched the animal channel like I did growing up and seen how lions hunt down huge water buffalo or zebra, you'll notice that the lion rarely attacks a whole herd. Ten out of ten times, this would be unsuccessful. Instead, the lion typically waits patiently until it finds one unsuspecting zebra that has separated from the group. Once that zebra is isolated, without any help, or any community, the lion has his way and successfully conquers the innocent animal. You may believe that you haven't done anything to anyone, and you are good to go, but I have to let you in on a little secret. The devil does not care. When you decide to go at things all alone and without any help, it is only a matter of time before the enemy has his way with you. But the good news is that God saw fit to give us a place and a system that can shield us, grow us, and mature us, and that is the body of Christ, AKA the church.

There is a story in Acts 8:26-40 about an Ethiopian eunuch. In this story, the Holy Spirit led Phillip to a desert, and, once he got there, he found a man who was sitting in his carriage reading. When he investigated further, he realized the man was reading what we know today as the Bible. The passage says, "So Philip ran to him and heard him reading Isaiah the prophet and asked, 'Do you understand what you are reading?' And he said, 'How can I, unless someone guides me?' And he invited Philip to come up and sit with him." (ESV)

This passage lets us know that you can be reading the word of God, appear to be a spiritual person, but yet still lack understanding. The man admitted that his understanding was limited and there'd be no way to actually understand unless someone guided him. This is true of you and I. God plants us in churches to give us shepherds or leaders who will guide us. If we reject the church and try to go at it all alone, unfortunately we are again depriving ourselves of a level of guidance and instruction that we so desperately need to grow and succeed. The church is monumental in our growth. Pray that the Lord will lead you to one that will feed you, equip, and empower you in the walk with Christ.

Chapter 5

Service

Exodus 8:1 (KJV) says, "And the LORD spake unto Moses, Go unto Pharaoh, and say unto him, Thus saith the LORD, Let my people go, that they may serve me." One thing we must understand as a believer now in Christ is that our salvation, while it was intended for our reconnection back to God, has other purposes. In fact, the most important factor in this equation is that we were actually delivered and saved to now serve God. Our lives were designed to worship and serve God in the intimacy of our relationship with Him. So now that we are newly born again, we must get back to the heart of our design, which is to serve God. Our salvation was literally predicated on our ability to serve. Service is our lifeline. Service is our duty. Service is and should be the DNA of every believer in Christ. Even Jesus, the Son of God, when he was here on earth, dedicated His entire life to service.

Matthew 20:26-28 (NIV) says, "Not so with you. Instead, whoever wants to become great among you must be your servant, and whoever wants to be first must be your slave—just as the Son of Man did not come to be served, but to serve, and to give his life as a ransom for many."

If Jesus himself lived a life of service, then how much more do we need to also be servants?

What is service? What does it mean to serve?

There are a few definitions for the word service which tell us that it is the act of assistance or help, but I'd like to submit to you a more in-depth definition. Service is the combination of both the willingness and ability to be used. Service is anything you do or any way you avail yourself to be used for the glory of God in any and every area of your life. The point of service for a believer is to be a vessel which acts as a conduit for the manifestation of God's glory and the advancement of His Kingdom agenda. When we look back to Exodus 8:1, the Bible explains to us that our salvation was that we may serve God—in some translations, it says to worship God. It stands to reason that our service is also our worship of God. If we are a people who only know worship to be singing slow songs in church but not as our service as well, then we are missing a key factor in our Christian lives. We must have a desire to serve God with our lives as an act of worship.

How do I serve?

Service to God comes in many forms. As you grow in your walk with Christ, you must ask the Lord to first give you the heart and desire to serve. Service is often limited to working at your local church, but it should be at the core of who you are and should be seen everywhere you are. Your service will never be accepted or validated by God if your heart is not for Him to begin with. As you begin to walk in service to God, whether in church, business, charity, or everyday life, do not see your service to God as a bribe to try to manipulate God to do things for you. Your service should be a genuine response to who God is to you and your desire for Him to be glorified. As a result of this heart posture and the obedience in action, God will begin to pour out certain blessings and results into your life. When you begin to serve, you must always place your heart in a place of humility. Your humility is what keeps you loyal to the work of God and produces longevity. The moment we allow pride to arise in our service, it becomes polluted and is no longer accepted by God. If you ever find yourself in a place where you begin to count all you've done for God and all you've done for people, the efficacy of your service is in jeopardy.

Biblically, the perfect blueprint of how to serve is found in 1 Samuel 12:24 (NIV): "But be sure to fear the LORD and serve him faithfully with all your heart; consider what great things he has done for you." Joshua 22:5 (NIV) says, "But be very careful to keep the commandment and the law that Moses the servant of the LORD gave you: to love the LORD your God, to walk in obedience to him, to keep his commands, to hold fast to him and to serve him with all your heart and with all your soul." These two scriptures show us very plainly that our service must be first in reverence to God and with all our heart and soul.

Serving in church

As we learned in the previous chapter, the church is God's program and institution that was designed to educate, build, train, and mature believers in the principles and systems of the Kingdom of God on earth. With this understanding, combined with the knowledge that the church is also the name we use to classify the larger body of Christ, we know each and every one of us has a vital role to play. This role we play is what I call service. If you go to any corporate organization in the world, especially those world-famous name brands, whether in clothing, food, or financial institutions, there is a name on them which we know, but behind the name are many people. The same is true with the church. We all come together to raise the name of Jesus Christ and, by serving in your local church, you have decided to take on the task of corporately exalting the name of the Lord.

Serving in the house of God is vital in the life of the believer. When you first come to faith, you may not jump into serving in the church because your primary focus should be to realign yourself back to Christ and His Word first. However, as you mature, your service in the house of God will be the key to your next level. There are usually several departments in any local church that one can find themselves being able to serve. This includes the usher department, cleaning, welcoming, music, and even media.

As you begin to press towards serving in the church, consider two key things as you go. Number one, try to find a department that aligns with your natural talents or abilities. Often, the Lord has given us certain abilities for the purpose of yielding it to him and submitting it for use in his house. Number two, allow your leaders, pastors, and elders to guide you. These are the men and women who are seasoned in the faith and are able to hear from the Lord concerning you. Therefore, they may be able to see where you best fit to serve based on the leading of the Holy Spirit. One thing to remember when it comes to service is that it is often not aligned with convenience.

The moment serving becomes convenient, you may need to reassess your service. Service is sacrifice. So before you serve, make sure you accept that the purposes of God outweigh the desire for your own will and convenience. Serving in church is a privilege. Never forget this. Serving in the house of God is a privilege. To be involved in the continuity and advancement of God's Kingdom here on earth in any way is not something to be taken lightly. You should desire to serve in church and find a dedication in your heart to serve with all that you are.

Benefits of service

As you serve God in His house and as a lifestyle, there are some benefits. While we don't particularly serve to get anything from God, we must know who God is, and one of the dimensions of God is a rewarder (see Hebrews 11:6) the Bible lets us know that God is a rewarder. That means while your salvation is a gift from God, there are certain blessings that are merited. Your commitment and service to God is one way you invoke those blessings. There are many benefits and blessings that come with service, but I want to just give you a few biblical points to hold on to, a few of which are found in Exodus 23:25-26 (NKJV): "So you shall serve the Lord your God, and He will bless your bread and your water." The first bene-fit of service found in this passage is the blessing of your bread and water (resources and productivity). This lets us know that as we serve God, He steps into his role as Abba, our source, provider, and sustainer.

The next benefit is good health. "And I will take sickness away from the midst of you." Exodus 23:25 (NKJV) Those who serve God cannot, by the authority of scripture, ever remain in a place of sickness or illness, as it is against the Word of God. If you are serving diligently and see prolonged sickness among you, you must begin to pray and hold God to this very word and let him correct your situation. The last one of the promises here that I'd like to mention is longevity. "I will fulfill the number of your days" Exodus 23:26 (ESV). As you are a servant of God, He is committed to making sure your life is preserved and fulfilled. He is always intentional about keeping you from any attack or plan of the devil to bring your life to an end prematurely.

Serving God is a secret weapon in the hands of the believer, but unfortunately the body of Christ has either lost the value of service altogether or the service has been tainted by wrong motives and heart postures. In any case, service is what can truly take you from glory to glory. Many of us may be failing to see certain possibilities we desire in our lives because we've failed to genuinely live from our hearts and serve our Lord, both in our lives and in His house.

Chapter 6

Sharing the Faith/ Evangelism

As the Lord has now begun to transform your life, it is important you do not keep your faith a secret. The Lord rescued you, pulled you out of darkness and death, and changed your life from ashes to beauty, and the reality is that not everyone has had the opportunity to receive that yet. Our families, friends, and many other people we know may be living destined for death, but God brought us out that we may lead them out as well. To be a true believer in Christ is to love what He loves, and God loves people so much that it is His desire that nobody perishes. He has now entrusted us to be the tools here on earth to spread the message of Jesus and what He has done to save us and bring us back to Himself.

Introduction to evangelism

Matthew 28:19-20 (KJV) says, "Go ye therefore, and teach all nations, baptizing them in the name of the Father, and of the Son, and of the Holy Ghost: Teaching them to observe all things whatsoever I have commanded you: and, lo, I am with you always, even unto the end of the world. Amen." This scripture is often used as the foundational scripture for evangelism. This command was given to Jesus' disciples right before He left earth and ascended to heaven. This was the command that is also given to every one of us who are believers in Him. With this scripture, we also see the value God has for people because this command was given so we would share this gift of salvation with ALL nations. The word nations can also be translated to "people", meaning that God desires every person to be reached. Understanding that evangelism is God's desire and one of His top priorities, we must now understand how to reach others.

What is evangelism?

Often when we use the term evangelism, it is used in a way that doesn't fully encompass exactly what it means and the goal of it in the first place. As a believer in Christ, we must continue to remind and train our minds to fully know the depths and dynamics of salvation and what it means to be saved. Evangelistic efforts often fail because there is not a thorough understanding of the gospel of Jesus Christ and how to communicate that to someone who has never heard of Jesus.

Evangelism is simply the word or term that is used to describe going out in the dying world and winning souls for the Kingdom of God. It is about preaching the Gospel that God sent his Son Jesus to earth who had no sin to take all of ours and die as a living sacrifice that we may be granted reconnection with our heavenly Father and eternal life. John 3:16 (NIV) says, "For God so loved the world that he gave his one and only Son, that whoever believes in him shall not perish but have eternal life." Before beginning to share our faith, we must know from beginning to end why we needed to be saved, God's plan for salvation and redemption, and His purpose for our being, which we talked about in chapter two. If we become students of the word, and really learn the full scope of salvation before anything, we will see the message and salvation of Jesus Christ reach and rescue more people in the world and in our communities. Learning how to articulate what you believe and how to best explain salvation is one of, if not the most important aspect of truly walking in the purpose God has for your life. For some of us, the elevation, connections, community, destiny helpers, and fulfillment of purpose are all connected to how diligent we are in sharing the freedom of Christ with the world.

If we revisit Matthew 28:19-20 (KJV) "Go ye therefore, and teach all nations, baptizing them in the name of the Father, and of the Son, and of the Holy Ghost: Teaching them to observe all things whatsoever I have commanded you: and, lo, I am with you always, even unto the end of the world. Amen", we must begin to break down this command and expectation of evangelism given to us by Jesus by following these steps.

1. A task for every believer. This is one of the few calls and tasks that Jesus gave to literally every believer. In fact, this was the very last thing He said to the disciples before he ascended into heaven. This means that evangelism and doing this work are not only limited to people who are called to be evangelists by office, or even an evangelism team in the church. It is our RESPONSIBILITY and an expectation given by God.

2. Go. The first word in this command is "go". Evangelism is not a stationary action. Evangelism is not something you do in comfort. To evangelize is to go. If you fail to go to your family, your workplace, your friends, on the street, or on social media, then you have failed to fulfill this command of Jesus. We must understand that if we don't go, many people will never hear the gospel and thus many people will die and their

blood will be on our hands. God expects us to do our part and bring the good news, but the good news may never arrive if we don't take it. Ezekiel 3:18 (NLT) says, "If I warn the wicked, saying, 'You are under the penalty of death,' but you fail to deliver the warning, they will die in their sins. And I will hold you responsible for their deaths."

3. Make disciples. The next part of the scripture (Matthew 28:19) is to teach the people and make disciples. This is the action that we've been talking about. This is giving people the good news, them hearing and receiving the word of truth, and committing them to growth in Christ through discipleship. Evangelism always has and always will be a twofold responsibility: winning souls and discipleship.

4. Baptism. The next step is to baptize these people. The conversation of baptism is extensive, but we must understand there are two types of baptism that we'll mention and that is first the baptism unto forgiveness, also called salvation and regeneration. The second is baptism by immersion in water. This form of baptism is the outward and physical representation of what has taken place within us spiritually. It is also an outward declaration unto God and before man to state that

you are on the Lord's side. The word baptism simply means to immerse. So anywhere there is immersion can be considered baptism. When this scripture commands us to lead people in this way, it means both baptism by water and the spirit—immersing people into the body of Christ, following Jesus, and helping them change direction in their lives.

5. Don't be afraid. The Lord gave us some encouragement, so we need not be afraid when going out to do such a large task. He tells us He will always be with us. At the end of verse 20, He says, "And be sure of this: I am with you always, even to the end of the age." So we know we are always covered. He has given us power, backing, help, and support to go and make sure that this message is spread at all costs. John 16:7 (ESV) says, "Nevertheless, I tell you the truth: it is to your advantage that I go away, for if I do not go away, the Helper will not come to you. But if I go, I will send him to you." By leaving earth and ascending to heaven, He was able to send a helper, His spirit, or the Holy Spirit, to comfort, help, teach, and guide us in life.

Knowing these things, we can boldly go out into the world and share the gospel.

Where do I start?

The question you may have now is, "How do I even begin to go about this? Where do I start?" Start right where you are, with what you have. Your first ministry should be your home, your family, and those closest to you. When God sent the disciples in the book of Acts, He said something very key in the order of evangelism in Acts 1:8 (NIV), "But you will receive power when the Holy Spirit comes on you; and you will be my witnesses in Jerusalem, and in all Judea and Samaria, and to the ends of the earth." This is key because when they heard this word, they were in Jerusalem. That means that Jesus expected them to start where they were and then work from the inside out. For us, too, the work must always start where we are first. With that being said, here are three simple ways to begin evangelism, no matter what level you are in your walk with Christ.

1. Share what you believe (Jesus as Lord and savior). This can include your testimony, but always explain how God sent Jesus to redeem mankind from death and sin.

2. Share scripture (Romans 3:23, John 3:16, Romans 10:9). These are key scriptures known as the Romans Road to salvation, and they plainly

let us know why we need salvation and what
steps to take to receive it.

3. Make clear the only way you go to heaven is
   through a belief in what Jesus did.

   a) Ephesians 2:8 (NIV) says, "For it is by grace
   you have been saved, through faith—and this
   is not from yourselves, it is the gift of God."

Sharing our faith is crucial in our Christian walk. It is not
a great suggestion, but it is a great commission. There is
a responsibility and an expectation to share the gospel
of Jesus, and we are encouraged and empowered to do
this work. As you begin to value and obey the thing that
is most precious to God, saving souls, God will begin to
make a miracle and a wonder out of your life. There is no
way that if you actively pursue this command that God
will leave your life the way it was when you first started
with God. He will completely beautify your life in every
way. The Bible tells us in Proverbs 11:30 (NKJV), "The
fruit of the righteous is a tree of life; And he that wins
souls is wise." It is wise to win souls because anytime
God's priority is your priority, so are His riches, blessings, abundance, and life. It is all committed to you. May
we have a desire to share the good news of Jesus Christ.

Chapter 7

Saved, Now What? (Conclusion)

We are excited about your journey with Christ. Indeed, accepting Jesus into your life, accepting His sacrifice, and choosing to live for Him is the best decision you could ever make. Our hope is that now that you've learned some key steps to take in walking out this life with Christ, that you feel empowered, equipped, and ready to excel in your life. All that we've shared in this book has simply been your starting off point. There is still so much to learn about God and with God, but with this blueprint, we trust you will grow and do wonders in the Kingdom of God. With that being said, we'd like to leave you with three final thoughts to take with you into your new life.

1. Remain teachable, stay humble

As you journey deeper and deeper with Christ, always remember to keep the heart of a student. 1 Corinthians 8:2 (NKJV) says, "And if anyone thinks that he knows anything, he knows nothing yet as he ought to know." This simply means the moment you begin to think that you've got it all figured out or, furthermore, you've got God figured out, that's the exact indication that you still have a lot of learning to do. We must aggressively fight against any mentality that we have arrived or reached a place where there is no more ascension to be made. This mentality is a form of pride, and we, as believers, must truly lean on the grace of God to help us overcome it daily.

In Christ, there is always a next level, as we never reach the point of having done it all or seen it all. In Revelations 4:1, the Apostle John heard a voice, even after being brought up into heaven, the actual place of God's glory in the spirit, telling him to *come up here, that I may show you things.* You would think the man is already in heaven, he's already reached the pinnacle, and what more could there be? Even in heaven there is room to grow and ascend, so how much more can we do here on earth as we walk out this thing called life? As you ascend and God begins to do mighty and miraculous things in and through your life, always give God the glory, never let pride poison what God has given you, and always carry a spirit of service and honor for all those whom God brings into your life.

2. No man is an island

Luke 2:52 (KJV) tells us our savior Jesus, while here on his earth, grew in a few different ways as he journeyed into purpose: "And Jesus increased in wisdom and stature, and in favor with God and man." The reality is that no one man is capable of fully walking out the call and purpose of God for their lives alone. God designed all that goes on in the earth to have to partner with mankind. Every blessing, help, and fulfillment of destiny comes from God, through man, to man. There will always be a partnership that must take place for God's will to be done on earth, and you won't always be the one who carries the torch. God has precisely designed us to be a body that has many different parts and functions. Knowing that we are a body, we must not isolate ourselves by any means and learn to actively collaborate and thrive with one another. The moment a part of the body gets cut off, it is dead. Don't be a dead Christian; stay connected to those whom God has set in your life to grow with and manifest the Kingdom of Heaven here on earth with. Great things happen when there is unity, collaboration, and teamwork. One can put one thousand to flight, the

Bible tells us, but two can put ten thousand to flight. We are always going to be able to accomplish so much more as a unified body of Christ, than an individualized, cut off body part. Trust God to bring you in connection with those who will help propel you into destiny.

3. Tell the world about Jesus

God is working through you now. He has chosen you and picked you for such a time as this. As a child of God, we must lead as many people as we can to Jesus. Never forget that it was never God's desire for his creation to perish and spend eternity away from Him; so we must do our part and share God's love with the world by telling them what Jesus did for us all. We know now that telling the world about Jesus is not just a command by God, but our responsibility as well. When you finally arrive in heaven when it is all said and done, after you have led many people to Jesus, you will see the abundance of treasures and rewards stored up for you. Heaven will rejoice and give a standing ovation for the work you've done for the Kingdom. As you prioritize sharing the gospel, the Lord will prioritize beautifying your life at all costs. Never be afraid to speak about or share Jesus. He promised us to always be with us and gave us the power to do so. Start right where you are with your family first, then your friends, and then spread to the ends of the earth.

This may seem like a big task, but nothing is too big for God. Lean on Him and He will see you through.

God bless you for reading this book! We pray that as you have availed yourself to know God and walk with Him that He will perfect all that which concerns you. He will keep you in perfect peace, deliver you from all evil, beautify your life, make you a sign and a wonder, and do great and mighty things in your life and your generations to come. It is our prayer that there will be nothing that can separate you from the love of God and nothing will drag you out of His hand. You will not fall back into the world. You will not go wayward. You will not live your life as an orphan, but you will live as a victorious and excelling child of God. With all that has been laid out in this book, take all the lessons, meditate on them, utilize them all, and share them with someone you know. Share this book with your new friends in Christ, with the person you told the gospel to, with your family, friends, and even your co-workers. Let this book be another tool you use to advance the Kingdom of God on earth, because just like you, when you began this book, many people still have the question, "I'm saved, now what?" May you be the answer that many are looking for. May your life, after reading this, be a walking blueprint for those looking to grow and know God. You came to this book with that question, but we want to ask you one back. Now that you know what comes after salvation, what are you going to do to manifest the Kingdom of God on earth? How will you contribute to God's glory being seen on earth? How are you going to be the beacon of hope and light in a dying world?

You are saved, Now What?

About the Authors

Jahred was born and raised in Baltimore, Maryland and Rukiya was born and raised in Brooklyn, New York. The two met in 2016 in Los Angeles California, both in pursuit of receiving their B.F.A in Dance Theatre. After knowing each other for five years, Jahred & Rukiya married and became 'The Rices' in 2021. Since being married they have dedicated their life to serving the purposes of God and preaching of the Gospel of Jesus Christ. To the glory of God they have been able to travel and win souls in many states throughout the east coast; New York, Washington D.C, Maryland and Virginia, just to name a few. It is their hope to continue spreading the gospel through books, social media, in-person events and any other way that will glorify God.